FOSSIL RIDGE PUBLIC LIBRARY DISTRICT

W9-BSC-102

Fossil Ridge Public Library District
386 Kennedy Road
Braidwood, Illinois 60408

10/00

DIRTY DOG BOOGIE

Written and illustrated by Loris Lesynski

Annick Press

Toronto • New York • Vancouver

FOSSIL RIDGE PUBLIC LIBRARY DISTRICT
Braidwood, IL 60408

For Dace, who helped make these poems sizzle.

©1999 Loris Lesynski (text and art)

Annick Press Ltd.

All rights reserved. No part of this work covered by the copyrights hereon may be reproduced or used in any form or by any means—graphic, electronic, or mechanical—without the prior written permission of the publisher.

Annick Press gratefully acknowledges the support of the Canada Council and the Ontario Arts Council.

Cataloguing in Publication Data

Lesynski, Loris
  Dirty dog boogie

Poetry
ISBN 1-55037-573-3 (bound)
ISBN 1-55037-572-5 (pbk.)

I. Title.

PS8573.E79D57 1999   jC811'.54   C98-932657-8
PR9199.3.L47D57 1999

Distributed in Canada by:
Firefly Books Ltd.
3680 Victoria Park Ave.
Willowdale, ON
M2H 3K1

Published in the U.S.A. by:
Annick Press (U.S.) Ltd.

Distributed in the U.S.A. by:
Firefly Books (U.S.) Inc.
P.O. Box 1338
Ellicott Station
Buffalo, NY 14205

Printed and bound in Canada by Transcontinental Printing, Montreal, Québec.

The art in this book was rendered in ink, wash and pencil. The text was typeset in Utopia, Klunder and Syntax.

You can write to Loris
at Annick Press,
15 Patricia Avenue,
Willowdale, Ontario
Canada M2M 1H9

Read them all alone
or
read them all aloud.

Read them to your Mumsy
or recite them to a crowd.

Change the words,
arrange the words,
or rearrange the beat.

Know a poem?
Show it off
to everyone you meet.

CONTENTS

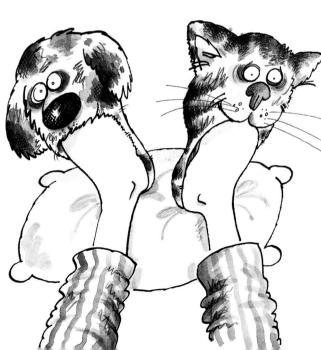

START HERE

A **boogie** is a dance

and a **boogie** is a jive

and a **boogie's** just another way of saying **I'm aLive.**

Boogie in an elevator.

Boogie in the street .

Anything's a **boogie** if it has a **buh**-buh-beat.

Boogie in a poem.

You can **boogie** when you're blue.

Boogie when you haven't got
another thing to do.

Boogie on your bicycle.

Boogie in your bed.

ALways keep a **bit** of boogie **going** in your **head!**

POE POE POEM RAH RAH RHYME!

4

YOU can DO one ANY time!
Top dog, bottom dog, doggie in between.
Rhyme about a dirty dog?
Rhyme about a clean.
ALL the body listens.
ALL the body hears.
A poem isn't oNLy
for your doggie little ears.

Feeling kind of crummy?
Run a rhyme instead.

ALways keep a bit of boogie going in your head.

ALways keep a bit of boogie going in your head.

ALways keep a bit of boogie going in your head.

Dirty Dog Boogie

I **had** a dirty dog
    and I **had** a dirty cat
and I **took** them both to
    the laundromat.

The cat objected
    and the dog complained
so I took them home
    in the pouring rain.

The cat got mad
    but the cat got clean
and the dog was as shiny
    as I'd ever seen!

So even though they yell
    and even though they yowl
I take them in the rain
    and I take along a towel.

If you have a dirty dog

and you have a dirty cat

don't take them

don't take them

don't take them to the laundromat.

SOS
(Send Only Sausages)

SAVE OLD SANDWICHES, SOS!

Send only sausages

S   O   S

we want sausages

and nothing less

mash the best potatoes

in the very biggest pot

serve them with the sausages

nice and hot

send only sausages

please send fast

without a lotta sausages

w e   w o n ' t   l a s t .

SEVEN ORANGE SALAMANDERS, SOS!

SLEEPING OVER SATURDAY, SOS!!!

Where the Sausage Rolls

The sausage rolls in the ocean
the sausage rolls in the sea
the sausage rolls in the frying pan
then it rolls around in me.

NOW THAT'S JUST **SILLY.**

8

Why...?

I did it because—

well the reason was—

it was really because...

because!

I did it because —

because everyone does —

because because because.

I did it I said it

I got it I get it

because because because—

because it was

what it was because.

Because **I don't know** because.

I Hate Poetry!

I hate poems.

I hate verse.

Nothing makes me feel much worse
    than the *ratta-ta-***tat**
of the pounding rhyme
    beat-beat-**beat**ing on me all the time.
Cat mat hat
    and *pink ink clink*
dump them all down the kitchen sink.
Teacher, teacher, what would you say
    if I read out loud at **you** all day?

I hate poetry.
I hate rhyme.

That's why I'm ending without one.

Monkeys

Merrily, hairily,
monkeys are mambo-ing
up to the ceiling
and down to the floor.
Thoroughly, furrily,
monkeys are shimmying
under the windows
and over the door.
Jumpily, bumpily,
monkeys waltz everywhere.
This monkey wallpaper's
hard to ignore!

Sunpuddles

Puddles of sun

    fill the living room floor

they spill in the windows

    and slide in the door

shining so hard

    on the tables and chairs

they melt just like butter

    and drip down the stairs.

CLoser to HoMe

Closer to home
    closer to home
        windshield wipers
            sssssssay
                sssssssssay

Wish
    we didn't have to go
        *wish*ing we could
            stay
                stay

Pouring rain
    Sunday night
        cottage *far* behind us tightly
            shut shut
                closed up
                    closer *to home*
                        to home

Spring a LittLe

Spring a little
spring a lottle
bring a couple
pop-a bottle
bike-a faster
snow-a go-a
picka-nicka
grass-a grow-a
spring-a leap-a
spring-a-bounding
spring-a time-a
run arounding

13

Laaaaaaaziness

LAAAAAZE

iness
    LAAAAAZI

   ness

      I have
         some
           of that
              I guess

     want to do
        a whole lot
         less

        don't much care
          my room's
           a mess

           s l o w n e s s
          gives me
            happiness

         kind of like my
          laaaaaayzeeeeenesssssssssssss

Mozza Mozza

Mozza

mozza

keeto

keeto

do not land-o

on my feet-o!

Do not sting-o,

make me twitchy.

I go "Ouch"y,

I go itchy.

Mozza mozza keeto **hey!**

MOZZA KEETO,

GO AWAY!!!

MOZZA MOZZA
KEETO KEETO
I AM **NOT**
A SNACK OR TREAT-O*!!!*

YUM!

Sock Fluff

Down in the corners of most of my toes,
  clumping together in bunches and rows,
right out of sight where it seldom shows
  — that's where I keep my sock fluff.

Blue socks make blue fluff
  and red socks make red.
Striped socks make some of
  each colour instead.
They stay in at night when I fall into bed
  —red yellow blue bits of sock fluff.

When I'm in the bath
    and the bits just begin
to start floating away from
    my soapy wet skin,
    I grab them …
        and dry them …
           and tuck them back in
—my favourite pieces of sock fluff.

Do ladies have sock fluff
    in ladylike toes?
Does everyone *else* have some
    under their clothes?
Or is it just *me* with this nice little cozy
    collection of personal sock fluff?

When I Was a Baby

Once I was a baby,
　　very small and sweet,
and Mommy planted kisses
　　on my tiny baby feet.

Ever since she told me this,
　　when I go out to play,
I say, **"Hey Mom,** how come
　　you didn't kiss my toes today?"

Bear
Toes

Bear toes

bat toes

thin toes

fat toes

bird toes

boy toes

girl toes

toy toes

wet toes

dry toes

stay off

my toes!

18

Unfffair

I can't spell **kat**

    and I can't spell **chairr**

I can't spell **appel** and

    I can't spell **per.**

But I can spell **rhinoceros**

    and **circumnavigation**

I can spell **kaleidoscope**

    caffeine

      and **fascination**.

Can I really help it

    if the words I spell the best

are never there

    among the ones

      that turn up on a test?

Fidgetfidgetfidgeting

(Background chorus: Fidgetfidgetfidgeting, fidgetfidgetfidgeting …)

OH NO!! My toe is fidgeting.
Oh ho! My leg is fidgeting.
And now my knee is fidgeting,
so all of me is fidgeting.

Fingers twitchy fidgeting
My face a-fitchy twidgeting
An antsy dancey fidgeting
I fidget everywhere.

But **wait**—my toes stop fidgeting…
and now my knee's not fidgeting…
My leg's no longer fidgeting…
now none of me is fidgeting.

Fingers still. *(No fidgeting.)*
Statue face. *(No fidgeting.)*
I take my place. *(No fidgeting.)*

No fidget
a n y w h e r e.

Housesong

My house is always humming
all the time all the time
with a whirry rumble-rumming
all the time all the time
if you listen—what a hissing
and a blurry sort of buzzing
house is full of growly fizzing
all the time all the time

Headsong

My head is always humming
all the time all the time
with a whirry rumble-rumming
all the time all the time
if you listen—what a hissing
and a blurry sort of buzzing
head is full of growly fizzing
all the time all the time

21

Wind

I don't mind getting rained on
    and I don't mind getting snowed on.
I don't mind getting frozen,
    but I **don't** like getting blowed on.

Wind! It pushes.
Wind! It shoves.
Snatches hats and grabs at gloves.
Bites my face with icy teeth.
Slips icy slivers underneath
    my longest scarf!
    my thickest coat!
Grabs me tight
around the throat.
    Blows so hard it knocks me down.
    Pounds and rushes all around.

Wind!

It rips and roars and swells.

Wind is how the weather yells.

Don't mind rain,

don't mind snow.

Just don't like

that *wwwwwind* to *blowwwwwww.*

Things in twos
are easy to lose
one of.

Pairs of socks
and mitts and shoes
I have none of.

23

Wet Feet

A Winter Chant

"How can **any**one be happy

when they've got **wet feet?**"

This is what I say as I go squishing

down the street.

(It always seems to happen when it rains or snows.)

How can anyone be happy when they've got wet feet?

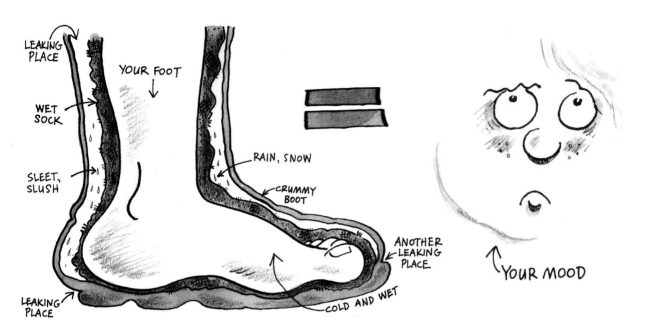

How can anyone be happy

    when their feet are soaking wet?

I stay away from puddles — but sometimes I forget.

    (My boots are very leaky, that's the reason I suppose.)

No one can be happy when they've got WET FEET.

    How can anyone be happy

        when their boots are full of sleet?

    No one can be happy when

        they've got wet feet.

        (Socks are very soggy when it's slushy in the street.)

NO ONE CAN BE HAPPY WHEN THEY'VE GOT WET FEET!

Why Won't My Boy...?

Why won't my boy wear his nice little mittens?

Why won't my boy wear his nice little hat?

  I know that he'll fit them

  I carefully knit them

from leftover fur that I found on the cat.

The Truth

Fretting mothers
JUST don't get it
just don't understand—
no matter what they say,
it's something true
throughout the land:
the undisputable, irrefutable
truth of the matter is **THAT**
some kids'd rather **DIE**
than wear a silly woolly hat.

DIED YOUNG BUT LOOKED COOL

Snowy Sunday with Homework

What is Toby doing?

Swimming in the snow?

He's a dog and not a fish.

Perhaps he doesn't know.

Diving in the snowdrifts

is the way he loves to play.

Toby doesn't have to do

a book report today.

(White cat
white snow
where did little
Spikey go?)

27

Can't Sit Still

No I **can't** sit still
never could
never will
gotta flip
gotta flop
gotta flap until
my bones are bouncing
my shoulders shake
with a jiggle and a wiggle
and I can't make me
STOP.

No I can't stand still
never could
never will
gotta jig
gotta jolt
gotta jump until
I've had enough of leaping
and I've had enough of hopping
and I'm thinking now of stopping
and **STOP.**

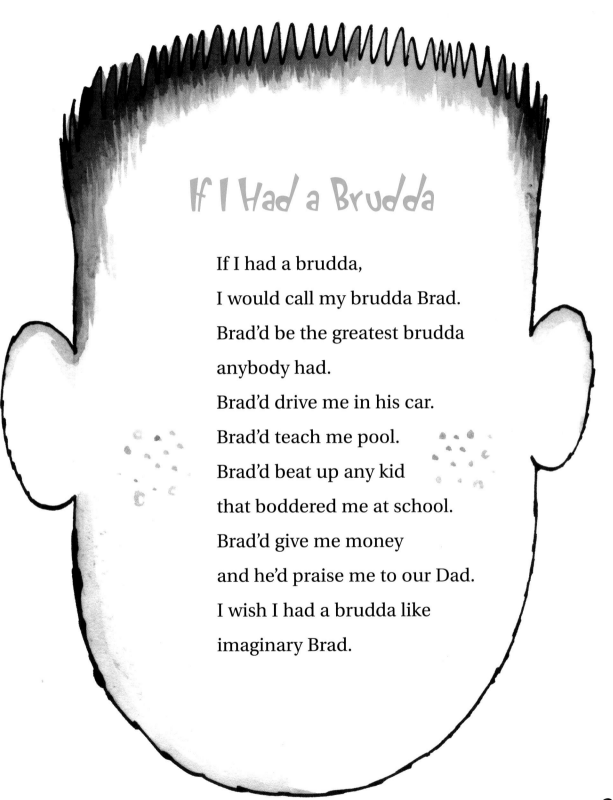

If I Had a Brudda

If I had a brudda,

I would call my brudda Brad.

Brad'd be the greatest brudda

anybody had.

Brad'd drive me in his car.

Brad'd teach me pool.

Brad'd beat up any kid

that boddered me at school.

Brad'd give me money

and he'd praise me to our Dad.

I wish I had a brudda like

imaginary Brad.

How I Lost My Appetite

I got a little appetite.
    It whispered, "May I have a bite?
A little lick, a little munch—
    oh please—just something
    nice for lunch?"

I gave it this, I gave it that.
    It ate it all in seconds flat.
It wanted more. "Of what?" I said.
    "Of everything!
    On buttered bread!"

I had a larger appetite.
    It gave my mother quite a fright.
It yelled, "I want a tub of jam,
    a dozen buns, a giant ham!
I wouldn't mind a thousand fries,
    and thirty-seven pumpkin pies."
It gobbled up the grub and grew,
    and cried, "I'd like spaghetti too!"

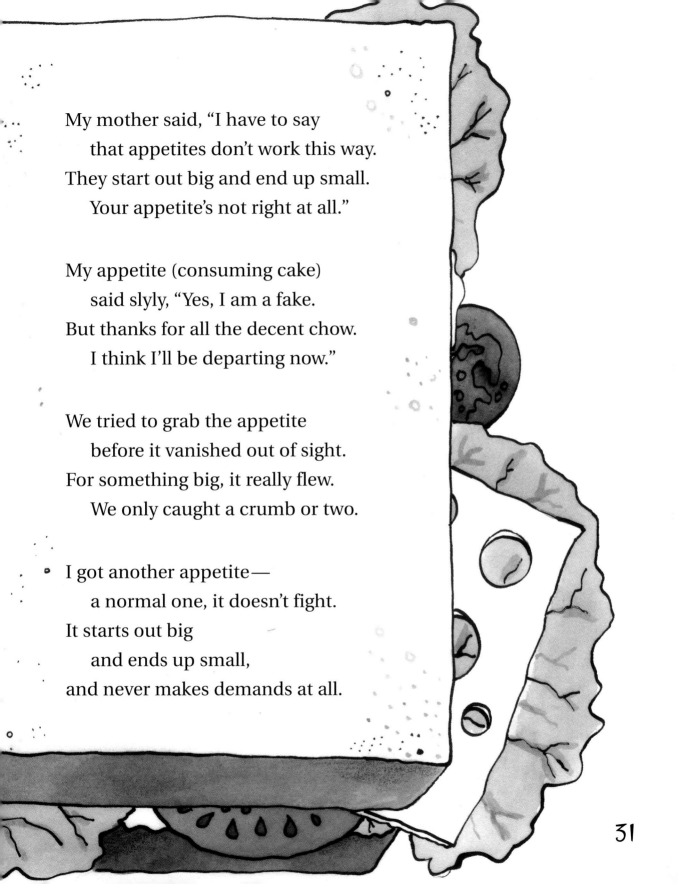

My mother said, "I have to say
    that appetites don't work this way.
They start out big and end up small.
    Your appetite's not right at all."

My appetite (consuming cake)
    said slyly, "Yes, I am a fake.
But thanks for all the decent chow.
    I think I'll be departing now."

We tried to grab the appetite
    before it vanished out of sight.
For something big, it really flew.
    We only caught a crumb or two.

I got another appetite—
    a normal one, it doesn't fight.
It starts out big
    and ends up small,
and never makes demands at all.

Nobody Knows

Nobody knows the troubles I've seen,
and gobody goes the gubbles I've geen.
Pobody poes the pubbles I've peen,
for fobody foes the fubbles I've feen.

When wobody woes the wubbles I've ween,
but bobody boes the bubbles I've been,
then thobody thoes the thubbles I've theen,
'cause kobody koze the kubbles I've keen.

3 2186 00109 4266

RIDGE PUBLIC LIBRARY DISTRICT
Braidwood, IL 60408

THE END